W9-CLW-053

# VESUVIO

## *THE STORY OF A VOLCANO*

Published by **KINA** ITALIA

# HISTORY

It is not difficult to imagine the kind of profound impression that the first adventurous navigators must have felt (probably phoenicians and then Greeks) when at the dawn of history they found themselves facing such spectacular scenery provided by a natural bay, surrounded by breath-taking limestone crests on one side and gentler projections of tufa on the other, and dominated by the unmistakable contours of a volcanic formation, the source of unknown and surprising phenomena, replete with atmosphere and mystery.
And indeed, that cone, Vesuvius' characteristic profile, set in the background of what would later become universally known as the Bay of Naples, became a loved and celebrated image even among the first, ancient inhabitants of what is one of the most attractive areas along the entire peninsular coast. Clear evidence that this was so has been found both in mural pictures and in the oldest literary documentation.
The last to be formed among the volcanic oreography of the Campania region, its origin has been placed by the experts amid the telluric formations of some twelve thousand years ago. The Vesuvius complex has certainly been responsible for the most disastrous eruptions witnessed by, presumably, vulnerable and terrorised prehistoric and early historical man.
Today, in the plain to the south-east of the parthenopean city, it is the only active volcano on the continent of Europe and certainly among the most famous and studied volcanos in the world. Yet in the classical period it probably did not provide any great reason for worry in a population settled at the limit of its slopes. It has now been geologically verified that it was then passing through a long period of tranquillity, at least starting from the VIII century BC. In addition it seems quite certain that at that time the highest point was somewhere around 2000 meters (as against the 1270 metres today) and that its slopes were covered with luxuriant forests and, lower down, by various types of cultivated crops, especially vineyards.
The characteristic and entirely unmistakable shape of the Vesuvian mountain, which has become a symbol of the parthenopean city and its region, is derived from the seismic transformations which the previous volcanic structure of Monte Somma underwent in that far off period. Geological investigations have indeed verified an alternation of explosive and effusive phases in this older formation: the primitive Somma, so-called by the experts in its activity set in the quaternary era, and the old Somma, dating back instead to the period between the seventh and the fourth millennium BC, experienced a sequence of eruptive periods with long intervening periods of calm.
In particular, at the same time as the period of intense activity in the nearby volcanos in the flegrea area,

PUBBLI AER FOTO

 *Panoramic area of the Gran Cono*

*Two eighteenth century prints which depict the volcano as it appeared at the time of the Pompeii and Herculaneum excavations*

Monte Somma gave no sign of life and on the contrary, following a progressive telluric lowering, it was even submerged under the sea. On re-emerging it reawoke with alternating phases until the first millennium BC, and enjoyed a long period of calm for a good eight centuries, until it was shaken in 79 AD by the terrifying eruption described in the celebrated letters of Pliny the Younger to Tacitus, in which among other things he gives an account of the tragic death of his uncle, Pliny the Elder, a notable naturalist and, fatally, an insatiable observer.
It was precisely that catastrophic explosion in the year 79 AD which, according to geological reconstruction, gave rise to the present Vesuvian outline with its large cone inserted amidst the remains of an analogous pre-existing and larger formation. The very numerous and more or less recent discoveries of inhabited settlements, some modest some of much more significant dimensions, made since the last century in the Campania territory in the lower slopes of Vesuvius, testify to a remarkable population density. This was of course due to the fact that the position faced the sea, as well as the mildness of the climate and the soil fertility.
Nevertheless, and sadly, the frequent volcanic eruptions which broke out over the centuries must have covered innumerable traces of man's presence in this region during the prehistoric period.
Later, in the historic period, there is evidence of peoples of Ausonian and Samnite origins, scattered among villages or in isolated farmsteads with largely agricultural and pastoral economy, with whom the growing power of Rome came gradually into closer contact.
Then, during the centuries of greatest splendour for the Eternal City, the area around the parthenopean Bay was the most densely populated in the Empire and, since the sophisticated and hedonistic taste of rich Roman society in the imperial period had countless and luxurious patrician villas built along the coast, vineyards and cultivation of Vesuvius' first foot hills certainly had to expand as a consequence, due to the growing appreciation by the Roman élite for the products of that

fertile land.
In the dark ages of the Roman decline and the barbarian invasions, characterised by a sharp demographic fall and by a general degradation of the agricultural countryside, the Vesuvian slopes obviously did not escape either, returning to wild and uncultivated land for many centuries. The only interval of relative tranquility in the area, and therefore also with a certain repopulation of the countryside, occurred with the imposition of the Longobard domination, in the VII century. The harsh tax policy and the centrist authoritarianism of the Norman domination, lead in turn and without interreption, first to the Angevin domination and then to that of the House of Aragon. All of which intensified the demographic crisis in the countryside, worsened by repeated and frequent famine and plague, driving the rural communities to flee, thereby overcrowding the urban settlements and abandoning the agricultural land to degradation and the encroaches of nature.
Only with the arrival of the Bourbons, and the start, in the XVIII century, of radical restoration programs in the plains surrounding Vesuvius, did there begin a significant repopulation of the area, concentrated nevertheless, and by preference in the coastal zone. Urban settlements of modest dimensions and prevalently agricultural and pastoral in economy, typical of the vesuvian slopes because of the frequent eruptions,have nevertheless always been held to rather low levels. And tucked away in the luxuriant green of the fertile fields on the volcano's lower slopes, almost always with the main façade facing the sea, there are the numerous (around one hundred and twenty, overall) Vesuvian Villas, remarkable examples of neapolitan baroque, built by some of the most prestigious names in Italian architecture: from Medrano to Canevari, from Sanfelice to Carlo and Liugi Vanvitelli.
And if today there is still a latent and potentially dangerous situation hanging over all the towns and villages in the area around Vesuvius, urban expansion and the tourist industry seem stubbornly determined to defy it.

# THE ERUPTIONS

In the eruptive history of the Vesuvian system four great periods have been identified, each one further divided into various sub-periods, these too, separated by more or less long periods of calm. The volcanic structure known today as Vesuvius is made from the formation created in the course of the fourth period, that is the present one. The cause of the volcano's returning to activity, occurring between pauses lasting many centuries, is attributed by the experts to an increase in the gaseous formations produced by the magma, following the mixing of original magmatic masses with sedimentary masses, within which there is the so-called "focus", that is, the centre of the burning material, located at a depth of approximately 5-6 kilometers.

Concerning the prehistoric periods there are obviously only hypotheses, formulated on the basis of studies and their related deductions. It seems probable, however, according to these investigations, that in the pliocenic period Vesuvius had a cycle of submarine activity and only later did it emerge from the billows, so to speak, and switch to its surface activity.

Certainly the eruptive displays in the prehistoric period must have been numerous and impressive : the evidence can be seen in the lavic formations still visible today on Monte Somma; the lava flows solidified on the lower slopes where, incidentally, Pompeii was built; and the numerous secondary cones which surround it (the most important of which is certainly that of Camaldoli).

In all probability the last eruption in the period immediately preceding the present one, that is the third period, must have been explosive and almost certainly created that majestic crater which today forms the rim of Monte Somma. This was subsequently extended, in a later phase of demolition, due to land slides and meteoric erosion, during the rest phase enjoyed by the volcano during the Roman period.

The experts date the start of Vesuvius' historical period with the famous earthquake in 63 AD, described by Seneca. This was probably a forewarning of the later and more terrible reawakening in 79 AD and we know that it had ruinous consequences for all the habitation centres at the foot of the mountain: from Naples to Herculaneum, to Pompeii and to Nocera. It was therefore this activity in 79 AD which constitutes Vesuvius' first historically documented eruption (described in the two famous letters by Pliny the Younger to the historian, Tacitus) sixteen years after the violent earthquake which had devastated the region.

This time too, the phenomenon first announced its presence with several preliminary tremors, but when, finally, the violence of the gas and the incandescent material succeeded in once again opening the subterranean channel the eruption exploded skywards with appalling power. One whole side of the mountain was torn away for a length of two kilometers hurling out a fury of scoria, sparks, boiling mud, poisonous gasses, lava, burning stones and ash.

This then was the precise moment when, from that lesion, the so-called "Grande Cono" was created, that is the picturesque crater which has stubbornly continued, up to the last eruptive phenomenon in 1944, to send up its unmistakable plume of smoke, a sight for centuries associated with the image of Naples and its Bay.

The eruption in 79 AD completely destroyed Pompeii, Herculaneum and Stabia, causing one of the most serious natural catastrophes in ancient history. The only naturalist to witness this frightening phenomenon was Pliny the Elder, who indeed finished as a victim to his insatiable investigative curiosity. Farther away, and decidedly safer, his nephew, Pliny the Younger, at Capo Miseno, also observed what was happening and, later, around 106 AD, he became its only official historian with what is the oldest written account of vulcanology - the two letters, that is, in which Pliny the Younger describes the details of the eruption with notes taken from those who had accompanied his uncle as well as everything he had himself seen.

From these documents it is possible to extract not only precious information that helps to scientifically reconstruct the phenomenon, but it is also possible to get an idea of just how terrifying and frightening it must have been for both witnesses and victims.

Equally significant for an understanding of the terrible desolation and the ruin left by the eruption is the famous epigram by Martial, composed by the celebrated latin poet in 88 AD:

*"This is Vesuvius, a short time ago green with vines;*
*here the golden grape had pressed against the wet vats.*
*This is the mountain that Bacchus loved beyond the Nisa hills, his homeland;*
*on this mountain the Satyrs threaded their dances.*
*This was the seat of Venus (Pompeii), more pleasing to her than Sparta;*
*this place (Herculaneum) was famous through the name of Hercules.*
*All lies buried by the flames and by a terrible conflagration!*
*Not even the gods would have wished that such a thing had been done to them!"*

And beyond the precise and detailed account by Pliny the Younger and the evocative verses by Martial, it is not difficult to grasp just how violent the eruption of 79 AD was when one considers that because of it the volcanic channel underwent a significant shift and the morphology of the contours suffered those distinctive alterations which have given it its present day form. Early iconography, indeed, (a fresco discovered at Herculaneum and two more discovered at Pompeii)

*Eighteenth century engraving of Vesuvius in an active phase*

*Effusive phase: the gases produced by internal combustion are emitted both from the crater eruptive channel and from lateral openings*

*Pages 12/13*
*Powerful sequence of images covering the past eruptive activity of Vesuvius, with emissions of gases, incandescent scorie and lava flows*

always depicts Vesuvius with a single summit and therefore before the split in the crater of Monte Somma. With regard to Vesuvian activity subsequent to the terrible episode of 79 AD there are only sporadic and flimsy reports; it seems that it can be characterised by what were for the most part explosive eruptions, with intervals of long periods of calm, sometimes lasting centuries. In 203 AD there was an eruption, but it did not cause any particularly serious damage.
A further episode, without damage or victims but of incredible power, occurred in 472, when the volcano vomited out its ash cloud as far as Constantinople and Tripoli.
Subsequent eruptions were recorded in 512, in 993, 1036, 1038, 1039, and in 1500, but all of them were of modest proportions.

A respite of more than a century preceded the catastrophic eruption in December 1631. An eruption which also announced the start of the true scientific analysis of Vesuvius, marked by an uninterrupted series of observations by the greatest scientists over the centuries in this research.
With deafening rumbles rising up from its depths, on the 15 December 1631 the volcano entered its eruptive phase and the following day its cone sent up into the sky a cloud that entirely obscured the sun
Immediately after, ten lava flows rolled down the slopes, while from the crater, mixed with ash, there were numerous explosions with enormous hissing masses. With unimaginable violence these struck Ariano Irpino, Avellino, Ottaviano, Nola, Lauro di Nola, Palma Campania, causing around four thousand deaths, apart

from the catastrophic destruction itself. The terror among the population was such that, as a chronicler of the time noted, they "thought the Last Day had come". And that conviction continued until February 1632, when Vesuvius, after having sent out a good two hundred seismic tremors and about ten sea-quakes, finally subsided.

In the history of Vesuvius the eruption of 1631 also marks the start of a profound change in its eruptive behaviour: the preceding discontinuity of activity gave way to a pattern of eruptive activity with a precise order. Within this pattern it was possible to identify two distinct phases, called respectively "rest" and "eruptive". The salient factor for these two is that in the first of these, and always following a violent paroxysm (a symptom of the close-down of a preceding eruptive period) the main eruptive channel is always blocked, while in the second phase it is almost always permanently in clear communication with the external environment.

The next reawakening of the volcano occurred in 1660, but this time there were no serious consequences and the damage was limited as it was in the eruptions subsequent to this at the end of the XVII century and in the XVIII century. In this regard the eruption of 19 May 1737 is worthy of note given that the lava invaded a good part of the inhabited zone of Torre del Greco; similarly with the one in 1779, when the crater spouted up a fountain of fire. Appropriately, on this occasion the abbot Galiani wrote his famous booklet entitled: "The very frightening description of the frightening fright which frightened us all on the evening of 8 August 1779, but which, thank goodness, did not last long."

Even today the bell tower of Torre del Greco has two storeys buried under the lava which invaded the small town in the later eruption of 1794.

Other lava effusions occurred in 1822, 1850, 1855 and in 1858. In 1861 it was again Torre del Greco which suffered the most serious damage, practically divided in two by the split caused in the overhanging slope. In 1872 the two inhabited areas of Massa and San Sebastiano were destroyed, while the lava completely surrounded the Vesuvian Observatory, seriously damaging it.

After just over five quinquennia the truce was broken in 1906. The mountain began its deafening growling in February. On the 28 of March its characteristic dark plume took on a worrying yellowish colouration and the inhabitants on the lower slopes were oppressed by a nauseating odour of sulphur. The rich, healthy cultivation spread over the surrounding territory began to progressively wither and, within a few days, the harvests were completely burnt. On the 5 of April there were the first earthquake tremors followed, two days later, by a considerable intensification in the frequency and violence of the seismic phenomena, while from the crater enormous burning masses were hurled to the sky. During the nights between the 7 and the 8 of April a horrifying torrent of incandescent lava began to descend along the side of the mountain, threatening first of all the hamlet of Boscotrecase: at the first building to collapse the inhabitants fled to the surrounding countryside, but around two hundred persons sought refuge and comfort in the church of Santo Spirito where, just as the parish priest was preparing to implore divine protection by celebrating mass, they were all tragically crushed by the collapsing roof, weighed down by the rain of ash and small stones. The Torre Annunziata too, was gravely damaged by eruptive material and the lava flow stopped just a few metres from the village. The emissions of rain of stones and ash continued for several days without respite, causing ruinous damage and subsidences in the whole area and in particular in the towns of Somma and Ottaviano. Finally, on the 21 April Vesuvius seemed to calm down. However, the violent paroxysm had meant an inner collapse within the mountain, changing its shape: at the summit indeed, there was now a craterous abyss whose initial capacity was calculated at around 84 million cubic metres. Vesuvius had, so to speak, been "decapitated" to the extent of some 180 metres.

At the bottom of this crater, in later years, there were repeated settlings which forecast subsequent eruptive activity and also indicated, approximately, the location of future openings of the eruptive channel.

Volcanic activity recommenced on the 5 July 1913, with an almost systematic succession of various phases: first, the repetition of eruptive pauses with the emission of only fumes; then the expulsion, more or less violent and copious, of scoria and lava fragments (with the consequent formation of a small, new cone, due to the accumulation of such materials); then the, as it were, disembowelling of the new small cone, generally accompanied by lavic emissions; and finally by a more or less ordered alternation of the two types of explosive and effussive activity until there was a gradual reduction in their intensity leading to a more stable condition.

From 1913 to 1944 there was practically an uninterrupted alternation of these different phases, with some variation in intensity and in the violence of the eruptive phenomena. In the first years, for example, after 1913, there was a gradual increase in the quantity of lava emitted in the various effusive phases, in particular in the activity during 1926, 1927 and 1928. The activity in 1929 was also accompanied by an explosive event of great violence, while those in the following year were relatively more moderate.

Overall, up to 1944, there was never more than a complete year passed by without lava emissions that

*Two eighteenth century engravings recalling Vesuvius' past volcanic activity*

*Pages 18/19*
*Sequence of images of Vesuvius in effusive and eruptive phases*

were more or less copious. One need only consider that over the whole period 1913-1944, the volume of lava poured out by Vesuvius has been calculated at some 250 million cubic metres, with a gradual decrease in quantity over this period.
On the 6 January 1944 there was an eruptive recrudescence which, with alternating phases, continued for about a month. After this it seemed to gradually grow weaker until, on 13 March, due to the obstruction of the channel following the collapse of the cone, it suddenly stopped. This phenomenon represents the initial point for a new pre-eruptive phase.
On the afternoon of 18 March, at 4 o'clock, the volcanic channel suddenly reopened with copious lavic effusions which, hurrying along the mountain lower slopes, destroyed a large part of the building structures and the cultivated lands: the worst hit areas were those of San Sebastiano al Vesuvio and Massa di Somma.
This first phase lasted up to 5 o'clock in the afternoon on 21 March and remains memorable for the quantity of lava ejected: about 21 million cubic metres in three days. Then came the so-called "lava fountain" phase characterised by the throwing up, repeated many times until noon on the 22 March, of impressive columns of incandescent material which reached and even surpassed a kilometer in height. The scoria expulsed in this phase, due to the violence of the phenomenon, reached 5 kilometers in height and, due to the action of the wind, was drawn into areas that were very far from the volcano's usual range of action: they even fell around Angri and Pagani, that is, more than 16 kilometers from the eruptive axis, to the south-east. Over the nineteen hours of the second phase, before the amazed eyes of observers, the incandescent fountain phenomenon was repeated eight times and while the first seven did not last longer than an hour, the last continued for over five hours. Then, after this somewhat forboding spectacle, there came, without the slightest pause, the third phase, called "mixed explosions" due to the incredibly varied nature of the material ejected, with a distinct predominance, however, of ash. The violence of the phenomenon was such as to raise spirals of dark and incandescent material more than 5 kilometers high and again due to the action of high altitude winds the fall-out reached areas at staggering distances from the eruptive axis: considerable quantities of ash, for example, fell in Albania, some 500 kilometers from the Vesuvian region. At 2 p.m. on day 23, the fourth and last phase started - the seismic-explosive phase: with variable intermittence and decreasing intensity, for six days the seismic and explosive activity continued. After day 29 there were only isolated seismic phenomena which, with variable intermittence, disappeared after about a year, while the explosive features definitively stopped at the end of March. In April 1944, during the allied occupation, the last element in Vesuvius' eruptive phase occurred. The last small cone collapsed into itself: the walls, no longer supported by the power coming from the inner energy, fell down for some 200 metres within and below the rim of the crater. Thus there was formed a vast concavity, on the summit, completely covered with yellow ash.
And from that day the famous, characteristic plume, too disappeared - what had been until that moment such an essential feature in the unmistakable image of the parthenopean bay.

▶
*A moment in the tremendous eruption in 1944*

# THE CRATER

*Section of the Vesuvian crater with indications showing the successive modifications to the eruptive channel in the period between 1906 and 1920*

*Page 21*
*The crater as seen from the Atrio del Cavallo during an effisive phase*

The volcanic countryside of Campania, divided due to its precise and different characteristics into four distinct complexes (the two large volcanic cones of Vesuvius and Roccamonfina, the vast aggregate of low-reliefs full of countless craters of Campi Flegrei, the scattered collection of volcanic islands which surrounds the bay of Naples and the adjacent coastline), presents both a variety and discontinuity which makes it particularly interesting.
And if the nearby Flegrei and island complexes reveal what are undoubtedly fascinating aspects both for the expert and for the dilettante or amateur, it is certainly Vesuvius which has always captured, over the centuries, the attention and general curiosity. In particular, its very distinctive shape has generated, always, investigations, studies and hypotheses (which have not always enjoyed agreement among scientists) as well as the most varied descriptions and interpretations of historians and writers. In effect very little is known about the form of the volcano before the historic eruption in 79 AD and the theory that the summit must have been different from the present shape (that is, with a single conical termination) - is based in essence on the examination of three frescoes, one discovered at Herculaneum and two at Pompeii, and on the descriptions of the historians Strabo and Floro.
While the two above-mentioned frescoes have been destroyed and today there remain only the precious evidence provided by two copies, the one discovered in 1879 in the so-called Casa del Centenario at Pompeii,

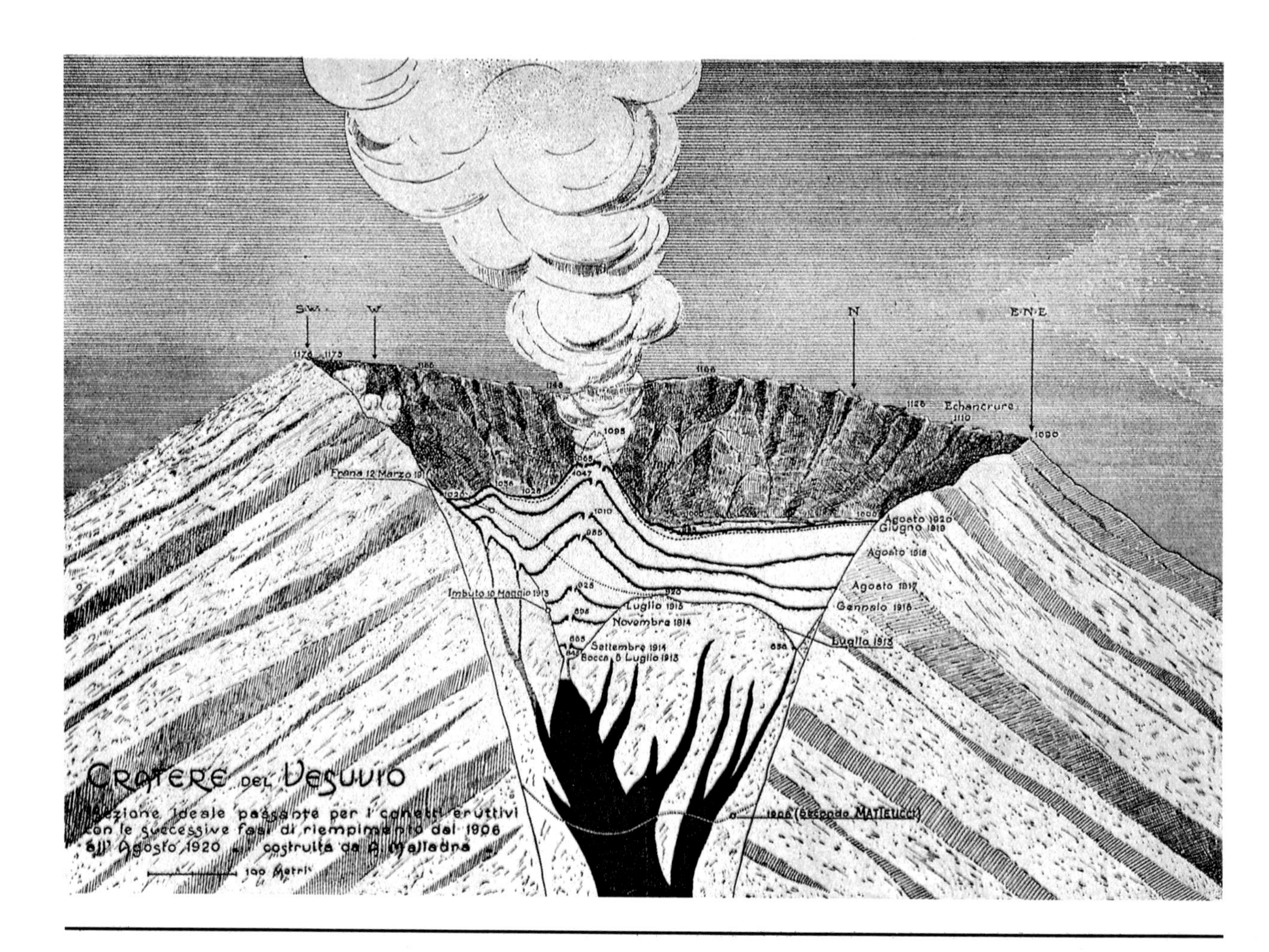

and at present kept in the National Archaeological Museum of Naples, constitutes the only original document of Vesuvius' former physiognomy: it shows an isolated mountain, with a single summit, at the foot of which there is the god, Bacchus beneath an enormous cluster of black grapes.
It is permissible therefore to suppose that the present morphology has been determined by the famous eruption described by Pliny the Younger, the one in 79 AD, and from that moment Vesuvius has assumed its truncated cone form, with increasing steepness towards the top and a robust and ancient crater border, at the centre of which there is the terminal cone, still today its characteristic feature.
The fact that the ancient crater wall was demolished along about half of its line was due to the violence of the explosion which reduced the apex of Monte Somma to a semi-circle: precisely that summit which, with the terminal cone, gives the volcano its two-headed shape as seen from Naples. The generic observation of the outline formation, apart from the scenic and historical interest, demonstrates the close relation existing between the external form and the eruptive character of a volcanic structure.
In effect, the experts have demonstrated how much the description of the eruptive displays, past or present, contribute to providing useful elements in the reconstruction of the original form, as well as the morphological variations suffered by the volcanic edifice over time due to the effect of its multiple constructive, destructive and simply modifying actions.
For example, in relation to the variations of the type of eruptive activity, it is possible to note a change in the average pitch of the external volcanic wall: when, that is, the effusive phases are in the ascendent, the average slope is relatively gentle, while the steepness is enhanced following explosive activity.
In general, however, almost all volcanos are of mixed origin and Vesuvius is no exception: thus from values that are quite low for the pitch at the bottom of its slopes, due to the presence, almost exclusively, of lava expansions, with an increase in altitude the slope

*Pages 24/25*
*Arresting image of the snow covered crater*

gradually steepens over all the intermediary slopes until, near the crater, there is the typical and steep rise due to the accumulation of fragmentary materials.
To gain a better understanding of its morphological structure and the reasons for its modifications over time it is also necessary to remember that Vesuvius is a pluriassic volcano: the channel, that is, through which the emerging masses supply its activity has almost regularly shifted, at its terminal extremities, along the same direction. And even if this shift proves to be relatively negligible (a few score metres over the course of several millennia), the most significant characteristic due to such a shift has been that of causing, during the renewed activity phases (generally occurring on the already blocked crater bottom, blocked since the conclusion of the preceding eruptive activities), the construction of new formations, which are thereby surrounded by the preceding crater walls or by the remains of these, if there have been partial destructions during the course of preceding paroxysms. This is precisely how the so-called "rampart volcanos" are formed - of which Vesuvius is the most classic prototype. Here the most ancient crater remains are constituted by Monte Somma, the new edifice is represented by the Great Cone and the intermediary valleys between the two is the Atrio.
At present the summit of Vesuvius culminates therefore in two differently shaped and composed peaks even though they are derived from a single common base, one to the north, made up of the remains of old crater walls now reduced to a kind of semi-circular bastion, the other to the south, whose centre opens out into the present crater. The perimeter of the entire volcanic edifice, measured at a height of about 50 m above sea level, is somewhere in the region of 40 km. The maximum height of Monte Somma, measured at its Punta Nasone peak (to the north of the Gran Cono), is exactly 1132 m, while that of Vesuvius properly called, on the peak to the north-east of the crater rim, is at present 1270 m.
Geological studies and morphological analyses have lead the experts to deduce that the ancient crater of Monte Somma must in the past have measured around

11 km in circumference. Very much reduced in comparison is the present Vesuvian crater, with a circumference of around 1.5 km. The geometric axis of the present crater has shifted by around 250 m with respect to the axis of the ancient crater of Monte Somma and this leads many to suppose that there has been an analogous shift due to their respective eruptive channels.
Starting from the west wall there is the beginning of a great depression, with its bottom almost flat, which starting from the Colle del Salvatore (where the Vesuvian Observatory is located) forms a kind of semicircle from the west to the north with the section called Atrio del Cavallo (that is the "saddle" dividing the peak of Monte Somma and the Gran Cono), to then proceed towards the east until it joins with the so-called Valley of Hell, where the barren walls of the Monte Somma merge into those of the mountain. This depression, called the Giant's Valley, is, like the Gran Cono, entirely covered by greyish sand and ash, with scattered traces of lava runs and heaps of brown-blackish lava. The highest point of the crater rim appears to be still buried beneath the explosive products from the eruption in 1944.
The subsequent land-slides on the crater rim, after the last paroxysm, produced not just a certain widening of

the rim itself, but also a distinct reduction in the crater's depth due to the amassing of all the detritus so that today it measures about 200 m.

*Fumarole during the active phase*

*One of the last of Vesuvius' "smoke puffs" while active*

# THE HISTORY OF EXCURSIONS AND CLIMBS TO THE CRATER

The undeniable fascination and the aura which Vesuvius' unmistakable form has always aroused both visually and in the imagination of the traveller make it highly likely that not a few bold spirits, even in far off times, decided to venture out over its slopes to discover its most hidden beauties and the most recondite secrets. If from the investigations of Seneca, Strabo or Pliny we learn of the most exciting events connected with the parthenopean volcano, from them too, as from many other texts on Vesuvius by writers from all periods, we can deduce the smallest and most detailed, and highly precious, pieces of information.
Apart from the epic tones with which Virgil immortalised the site, in his description of Aeneas' descent into the Sybil's cave, the image of Vesuvius which comes to us through the historical account of the flight of Spartacus and his followers is much more down to earth. They were encamped on the mountain slopes in 73 BC during the Slaves Rebellion. The Roman praetor, Clodio Pulcro, at the head of three thousand soldiers, had taken up a position along the only access road then known to the mountain and awaited the rebels at its opening. The slaves appeared to be finally trapped. The latter, however, exploiting the projecting cliffs on the south-east slope, dropped down one by one to the plain, helping each other with ladders made from the branches of the wild vines with which the volcano was particularly rich; hurtling down so unexpectedly on Clodius' camp, without the Romans having noticed anything of the manoeuvre, Spartacus' rebels routed the republican legions.
In addition to the detail here on the lush natural vegetation which can be gleaned from the narration of this historical event, it also tells us explicitly about a road which wound along the mountain sides and it is therefore a valid deduction that climbs to the top of the summit were not unusual events, even in those days.
Later came the dark years of the High Medieval period, with demographic decline, the abandoning of the countryside and the dangerous condition of the roads, all of which must have made those places much more wild and solitary. Certainly the access road to the volcano summit, noted in those ancient times, underwent the inevitable deterioration of every road that is no longer regularly used. Not until the Renaissance and humanist period did men, albeit experts or simply highly curious individuals, feel suddenly filled with a desire and an ardour to know and explore. And certainly Vesuvius was among the phenomena which most excited the interest of the human intellect. But the large smoking cone had to wait still longer, until the XVIII century, when, following the land drainage schemes for many marshy areas at the foot of the volcano, and the vast works of territorial improvements together with the reordering of

*Until the last decades of the nineteenth century the climb up the slopes could only be done either on foot or on horseback*

*Pages 30/32/33*
*Three ironic period images which clearly show the spread of the nineteenth century fashion for excursions on the slopes of Vesuvius*

*An image of one of the first Circumvesuvian vehicles*

the road network (and in consequence, the significant increase in the population), its slopes were once again lined with pathways, routes that were increasingly less narrow and solitary, more and more used by the eager and curious for their excursions.
And there were not a few, among the many visitors, famous individuals who, attracted by the fascination of this fiery mountain, wished to climb its flanks gaze into that final, (terrifying and insidious) abyss. They have left us a precious literary evidence of their experiences. Right at the end of the 18th century, for example, during that long itinerary which eventually embraced the whole peninsula, reworked later by the poet into the volume entitled "*Travels in Italy*", Wolfgang Goethe climbed Vesuvius no less than three times. He was driven especially by his naturalistic interest in such an unusual and varied environment.
In the last century the bands of excursionists were increasingly frequent and the climb to the volcano crater was, according to the chronicles of the time, one of the classic distractions sought out by the languidly bored Campania nobility scattered over the countryside in their splendid villas. Soon these too could be seen in greater numbers on the slopes. Then again it afforded the tormented parthenopean middle classes a rare chance to seize an opportunity for a moment of enjoyable escape. There is a magnificent description of the climb to Vesuvius' crater by Antonio Stoppani, the Lombard scientist and writer (as well as reunification patriot), in his book, "*Il Bel Paese*", published in 1875. In it he pointed out the stimulus given to the formation of a patriotic unitary consciousness by looking to the

common good of all the natural beauties in the peninsula.
There is no doubt that with the passing of the years, with the further exploration and clarification of the researches into the origin of the volcanic phenomenon, there grew, at the same heady rate, man's confidence in this natural structure and the climbs to the crater rim became almost a habit, even in periods of clear increase in its eruptive activity. And sometimes such confidence went tragically beyond all prudent limits, as when, during the eruption of 1872 which destroyed the villages of Massa and San Sebastiano, numerous excursionists were overrun by an incandescent lava flow in the Atrio del Cavallo, as they pushed forward to observe the phenomenon from a dangerous and ultimately tragic closer distance.

As incisive as it is suggestive, there is also the poetic image of Vesuvius left us by Giacomo Leopardi who, at the foot of the slopes of that "...formidable exterminating mountain, Vesuvius...", studded with broom and visited more and more, spent the last years of his tragically short life.
For a long time now the excursions to the volcano and the climbs to the crater have become an obligatory sight and attraction and a fundamental attraction for every tourist trip or program in the parthenopean area. And until around the mid 19th century the route was one of the most adventurous and accident prone (the chronicles of the time record clashes between police and brigands who had taken refuge in the thick Vesuvian wood, in 1863), since it was necessary to go on foot or horseback along the interminable mule tracks which zig-zagged

their way up the south-east or south-west of the Gran Cono. In the last section especially, the track went through intricate with razor sharp lava flows or skirted treacherous quicksand, on a slope that went steeply upwards at an incline varying between 50% and 70%. In 1873, no doubt to the great relief of many, the first cable railway was inaugurated.
The Vesuvian railway was, even in the first decades of the 20th century, destroyed on numerous occasions due to the volcano's effusive activity. It started its climb from the hamlet of Resina and went up for some 5 kilometres till it reached the Power Plant building at the foot of Monte Somma. From here, an electric locomotive on triple rails continued up to Eremo, near to the Observatory and, beyond this, as far as the lower cable railway Station. Taking the latter, the traveller reached the upper Station, a short way from the crater rim.
The repeated damage suffered and the subsequent repair operations modified the route on many occasions along with the positioning of the Stations on the mountain slopes, until it was finally decided to abandon the line altogether.
Today, it is possible to make the climb to the summit of Vesuvius from various points at its base. The most convenient ways are made up of the two roads which make the climb, one to the west from Pugliano (a more internal fraction of Resina) and the other to the south from Boscotrecase; at the end of these, easy paths lead directly to the crater. It is also possible to make the climbs from other directions too, but only on foot: from Torre del Greco and from Ottaviano.

*Detail of a typical "ropy" lava formation*

The Circumvesuvian Railway makes a complete circuit of Vesuvius' base at a modest altitude, allowing the tourist to thereby enjoy the extensive and complete panorama across its slopes. Still today it is a convenient communication route for the localities from which excursions can be made to the volcano's summit: for example, Resina-Pugliano, Boscotrecase, Ottaviano and Somma Vesuviana (from the latter it is then an easy task to reach Punta Nasone, Monte Somma's highest peak). The road starting from Resina-Pugliano is the most convenient and popular to get to the crater. After 13 kilometres in constant ascent, at about 830 m, the road splits into two branches: the one on the right leads to the nearby Funicular Lower Station which goes right up to the crater; the one on the left goes instead towards the Atrio del Cavallo, tempting the tourist to reach the crater on foot. Choosing the second is certainly the most evocative route: the last section is in fact made up of a path which winds along the precipitous sides of the crater, amid lava of various periods, in a desolate and unique environment. But this last section cannot be followed without the accompaniment of an expert guide so as to avoid the undeniable risks lying concealed in this extraordinary scenery.
While the route on foot requires about a half-hour to accomplish, the chair-lift means the last section can be done in just a few minutes. On arriving at the Upper Station, at an altitude of some 1160 metres, the crater rim offers, suddenly, a powerful sight, well worthy of Dante's Inferno. The numerous fumaroles shooting up out from the higher sections of the internal walls, with temperatures that can (on the north-east rim) even reach 500 °C, give a clear idea of the kind of power which still lies hidden in the depths of this seemingly sleeping mountain.
Particularly interesting, even if suitable only for the most expert and secure walkers, is the route going around the whole crater rim : the path has sudden and steep gradients and not infrequently it can, without warning, slip away for short sections. If, however, it is followed with the required precautions, the path makes it possible to acquire the most complete view of the Vesuvian summit: from the Atrio del Cavallo to the terrifying Valle dell'Inferno, where the bare walls of

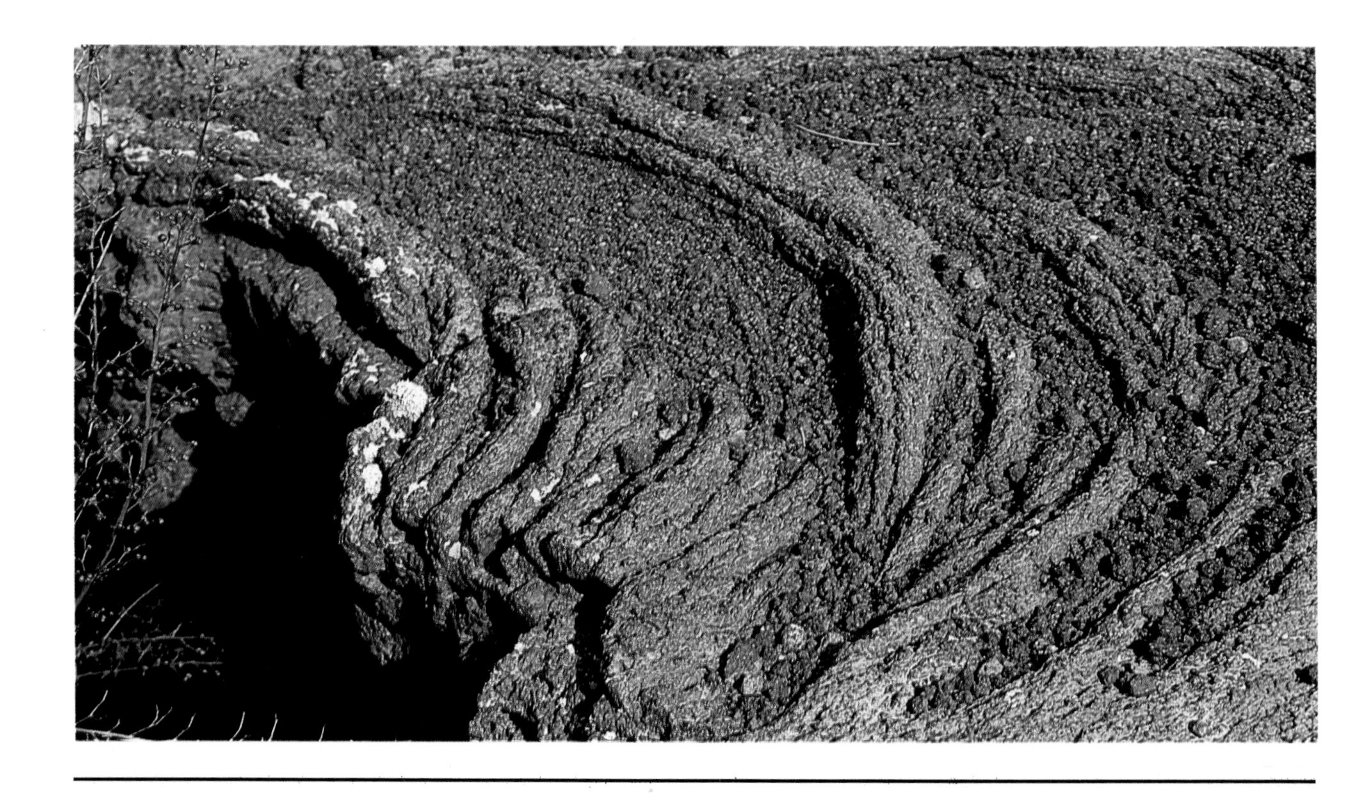

*Two moments during the climb to the crater*

*Pages 36/37*
*A group of tourists on the Colle Umberto, in front of the Gran Cono. On the left: some views of the route running from the Colle to the crater, across the Atrio del Cavallo*

*Detail shot of the Monte Somma crest, a particularly arduous route*

*Detail of the path making it possible to descend into the interior of the crater*

Monte Somma fall vertically away, riven by prehistoric lava flows. In around a half-hour, with this trip, the highest point of the crater rim can be reached, that is, 1270 m, completely covered with the 1944 eruptive scorie.
But the desolate, horrid spectacle inside the crater, however fascinating it may be, cannot obscure another, different spectacle which, as soon as one gets down from the Upper Station of the chairlift, can be seen by the visitor: from up there the eye, quite enchanted, can gaze round a full 360°, over the whole Bay of Naples, from Capo Circeo to Sorrento, and, towards the interior, over the modulated outline of the appenine crests, from Maiella to Monti Lattari, while closer, at the foot of the mountain, there are the green agricultural fields of the Campania countryside blithely rolling away.
As has been said, in addition to reaching the crater from Resina-Pugliano it is also possible to start from Boscotrecase, from which there starts the so-called "Strada Matrone", a convenient road which is in constant ascent as it winds its way through the very varied countryside. On the south-east side of the mountain it passes first among the luxuriant vineyards and a dense pine wood; then it penetrates into the

desolate spectacle of the lava flows stratified over the centuries and overall offers a stupendous view over the Sarno plane and the coastal strip running from Torre Annunziata to Castellammare.
Another station from which to start the climb to the crater is Ottaviano. From this hamlet it is possible to reach the forest path, a route that is longer than the previous ones but with naturalistic points of interest that are particularly worth seeing. It is a kind of surrounding rampart running for some 20 Km which winds along the south-west flank of the mountain, passing through marvellous chestnut woods and unsuspected picturesque angles until it reaches the Strada Matrone and then climbs to the crater.

# THE VESUVIAN OBSERVATORY

*A view of the new Vesuvian Observatory building and the surrounding garden*
*Above and rigth : plaque commemorating the construction of the Observatory*
*Below and to the left: the scientist, Vittorio Raffaele Matteucci, at the entrance to the Observatory*
*Lower right : Monument dedicated to Antonio Matrone, inventor and promoter of the road that goes up to 1000 metres*

On an isolated knoll of the west flank of the Vesuvian mountain, at around 608 metres above seal level, a verdant oasis in a desolate stretch of old and recent lava, there is the impressive construction of the Vesuvian Observatory.
A building in pure neoclassic style, designed by the architect Gaetano Fazzini, it was commissioned between 1840 and 1845 by Ferdinando II di Borbone, the King of the Two Sicilies who, revealing himself to be, in some senses at least, a considerably enlightened monarch, promoted outstanding reforms both in the economic and social field and in the scientific context, despite his pronounced political conservatism. A man of culture, particularly attentive to the affirmation of new positivist ideas, he showed himself to be sensitive to the need for more advanced study groups and systematic observations concerning the parthenopean volcano, and vulcanology in general.
It is an elegant building, surrounded by a magnificent garden, rich in all the characteristic species of the Vesuvian flora. The Observatory was built according to advanced architectural criteria, unusual at that time, which have made it particularly solid, able to resist the habitual seismic and eruptive activity of the mountain, that is, the telluric movements of relative intensity, the hail storms of lapilli and the ash storms. The first director of the new institution to be appointed was the celebrated physicist, Macedonio Melloni. He directed it

FERDINANDO II REGE
AB INCHOATO EXTRVCTVM
ANNO M DCCC XXXXI

VESUVIO
RICORDATO COME IL PIONIERE
DELLE STRADE VESUVIANE

*The spectacular panoramic view of the coastline from the Vesuvian Observatory*

*View of the Observatory's main façade with the tower*

*One of the most spectacular examples of Vesuvian flora, growing in the Observatory garden*

from 1845, the year of his inauguration, only till 1849, the year in which he was relieved of his duties due to his clear liberal sympathies and his declared support for the risorgimento and unification ideas in general. His successors were always notable experts and sometimes men of outstanding fame: from 1856 to 1896, for example, Luigi Palmieri was the director of the Observatory. During the 1872 eruption, although surrounded by incandescent lava, he did not want to abandon the building and remained there to observe "live" the electric phenomena which could be measured due to the enormous quantities of falling ash which indeed obscured the sky. The repeated, continual bulletins sent by Palmieri to Naples during the whole eruptive phase helped to control the situation and above all to calm the population.
Vittorio Raffaele Matteucci too, head of the institute from 1902 to 1911, was later remembered as the hero of the 1906 eruption. Indeed, in his attempt to verify from close up the activity of certain phenomena in the full activity phase he was hit in the knee by a mass of incandescent material and, later, died due to the damage suffered from by the eruptive environment. The famous vulcanologist and seismologist, Giuseppe Mercalli, too died a victim of his indefatigable interest in these studies and in the "live" observation of its related phenomena. He analysed in a particular way Vesuvius' activity and directed the Observatory from 1911 to 1914. After this the management was entrusted to four professors from the University of Naples, chaired by the director of the

*With the passage of time vegetation can even gain a hold on the magma: algae, lichens and especially broom*

Institute of Terrestial Physics. Later, around 1926, the specific and one-man direction system was restored and improvement works were carried out on the building. These were necessary because of the damages caused over the years, that is, due to the neglect of man rather than the fury of Vesuvius. Already in 1914 the building had been restored for the first time: the ash rains and storms and the earthquakes had undermined the walls and split the vaults, the particularly corrosive volcanic acids had destroyed the scientific instruments.
Later, the Observatory management extended even the organisation of its work in a more complete and systematic direction: while at one time Vesuvius' activity was followed only during the eruptive phases, today the volcano's life is unremittingly studied. In addition meteorological and seismic observations are carried out, clinographic and gravimetric measurements, studies into the atmospheric electricity and terrestial magnetism. The canopies used to make the magnetic, electric and gravimetric measurements are situated in the Observatory garden, the metereological apparatuses are in the highest area of the tower, whilst the underground areas are reserved for the seismological and clinographic apparatuses.
The easiest and most comfortable road to reach the Observatory is the one leaving Resina which then makes for the Lower Station of the chairlift. Besides the undoubted scientific and historical interest offered by this visit, the splendid panoramic view obtained from this position is not to be missed, covering as it does the whole flank of the mountain and the very intricate and varied physiognomy of the coastline.

## FOSSO VETRANA

The beautiful panoramic road running from Resina to the chairlift Station, immersed in the varied and changing green of the Campania vegetation in the lowest section, at a certain point, just before the Vesuvian Observatory, crosses the so-called Fosso della Vetrana. This is not a very extensive but rather a curious and impressive route due to the sudden scenery changes which the tourist can see. Running along the west flank of the mountain, the Fosso is characterised by the different lava formations along its route: those which came down during the 1872 eruption and the lava flows between 1895 and 1899, for the effusive emissions which were not accompanied by paroxystic phenomena, marked by exceptionally beautiful rope-like conformations which are rich in large leucyte crystals. The startling contrast with the vegetation below, so close and so luxuriant, whereas here it is already somewhat sparse, makes the Fosso della Vetrana a particularly noteworthy and impressive section of Vesuvian scenery.

*Detail which shows the modifying action of the lava flows on the area*

## COLLE UMBERTO

Volcanism in it multiple manifestations gives rise to a large variety of formations, some due to the erosive actions others directly emitted by the volcano. Among the latter, a distinction can be made between those of an effusive character and those with an explosive origin. The effusive formations are constituted exclusively by materials emitted directly from the terminal mouth of the volcano or from separated fissures along its flanks and, according to the shifts they undergo due to the viscosity which characterises them, they can accumulate around the mouth from which they sprang, forming a king of dome, or they can push their way out, even to a remarkable distance, in the form of lava flows of varied thicknesses.
One of these dome formations, formed during the interval between 1895 and 1899 on the western Vesuvian slope, is the Colle Umberto, a hill with a distinctively rounded profile, some 200 m high, which with the Colle Margherita (not for from the above, but more within the Atrio del Cavallo) represents, in fact, a typical example of a massive lava dome produced by slow and lateral effluxes of dense and macro-crystalline magma consolidating to form a united surface, with curious tress formations, characteristic of ropy lava. Though it was formed in just four years, with around 100,000 cubic metres of lava, the Colle Umberto is today the most resistant bulwark defending the Vesuvian Observatory.

## MONTE SOMMA

At the apex of the Vesuvian mountain there are two peaks which make its physiogmony unique and quite unmistakable: one of these is Monte Somma, a kind of semicircular bastion made up of the northern remains of old crater walls whose southern section, completely disembowelled, is today covered with stratified materials from the subsequent eruptions. The crest of Monte Somma is thin and has a highly jagged rim, subject to continual landslides. The highest point is that of the Punta Nasone at 1132 m, and difficult to reach due to the dangerous nature of the very narrow passageway.

## ATRIO DEL CAVALLO

Set amid scenery which seems ever more desolate and striking to the tourist, the Atrio del Cavallo opens up at the summit of the volcano after the climb through the wooded slopes of Monte Somma. The Atrio is a valley lying between the surviving summit of the Somma and the Vesuvian crater, offering the first powerful view of the overall complex, the Gran Cono. It takes its name from the fact that at that height the traveller has to abandon any riding. At about 1000 m high, the walk becomes more arduous due to the mobility of the layers and the very small lapilli.

**VALLE DELL'INFERNO**

The depression between the two crater rims continues towards the east in a section of the Atrio del Cavallo that is even more barren and rough underfoot: this is the horrible Valle dell'Inferno towards which the bleak and precipitous walls of the Monte Somma hurtle down, shot through with prehistoric lava flows.
The desolate, leaden scenery characterising this spot makes it quite clear why it was given its name.

# THE MUSEUM

The special "love-fear" relation which has always linked the parthenopean population to Vesuvius has over the centuries generated an attitude of caring attention with regard to what Neapolitans today good-naturedly call, "the mountain".
Despite the ruinous destruction which, over the course of history, the volcano has repeatedly caused to the surrounding areas, the inhabitants have never given up the task of repopulating its slopes, retracing their steps over the higher slopes, and watching its behaviour, storing their memories of it.
The observation of the volcanic activity and the conservation and documentation of its displays and its effects have been, at least up to the last century, due exclusively to the passion and interest of individuals, provided with individual means and entirely empirical in nature.
Only with the setting up of the Vesuvian Observatory, between 1840 and 1845, was there an organisation capable of studying the phenomenon in a more ordered and systematic way, based on strict scientific criteria.
No longer were just the exciting displays of the volcano taken into consideration but all its structural characteristics, including the materials emitted and stratified.
And still today, on the first floor of the Observatory building, there is a precious collection of Vesuvian minerals.
But only in our century, thanks especially to the studies by Giovanni Battista Alfano, has the investigation of the Vesuvian phenomenon become more detailed and rigorous. This famous vulcanologist, during his lifetime, unceasingly extended and completed the analysis of the seismic and eruptive activity of the mountain, and above all, the materials generated by such activity. On the basis of their composition and conformation, he arrived at a systematic and ordered classification of the various phenomena and their related products.
Having establisched, following the fractures produced, that orogenetic movements favour the upward movement of deep semifluid magma which, expanding on the terrestrial surface, causes effusive rocky formations, Alfano then identified the various activity periods on the basis of mineralogical and chemical analysis. The constituent elements
in the magmatic rocks are to a large extent made up of silicates, combined in different ways with aluminium, iron, potassium, calcium and sodium, distinguished by precise and specific crystallisation processes: in the recent ones, for example, there are lava products like liparites, trachytes, basalts and leucytes; in the older ones, there are instead mainly quartziferous porphyry, porphyrites and melanites.
In identifying, on the basis of this analysis, the different materials produced by the volcano in its four phases (trachytes and pipernoid tufa in the first, leucyte basalts in the second, again leucyte basalst in the third and leucotephrites and vesuvianites in the fourth), Alfano did not just examine Vesuvius with the same unceasing dedication due to a dear and particularly grave patient, but also spert his life meticulously collecting, storing and classifying a very considerable number of and classifying , a very considerable number of findings and documents on the various eruptive activities.
On his death that precious material, enriched even with more recent discoveries and by documentation instruments of various kinds, was collected and ordered in the Vesuvian Museum and named after this passionate expert of the parthenopean mountain.
An absolute must for any informed program for a complete visit to the Vesuvian world, the Museum is situated in the modern hamlet of Pompeii, not far from the sanctuary of the Madonna del Rosario, the famous basilica founded in 1876 and completed in 1939 around a renowned, miraculous image of the Madonna.
Of particular interest among the various collections in the Museum, there is the section dedicated to the minerals which have emerged from the volcano. In their variety of forms and colours the different examples of vesuvite, the silica mineral typical of Vesuvius, are particularly worth noting. These can take the form of prismatic crystals and sometimes even pyramid forms. The colour varies from brown to various shades of green, to yellow, red or sky blue.

*Above and moving to the left, several precious minerals kept inside the museum : Olivine, Sulphur, Calcite, Pink quartz, Red lava, Vesuvianite, Celestine, Pyrite, Mimetite, Hematite, Pumice, Black mica, Amethyst, Obsidian, Biotite*

# THE NATURAL PARK

The oldest story of Vesuvius has its roots buried in legend, but one fact has reached us without any hint of uncertainty even from those so distant times: the mountain and its surrounding soil, precisely because of its volcanic nature, were prodigiously fertile.
Some two thousand years ago, before the terrible reawakening that caused the destruction of Pompeii and Herculaneum, and after a certain and prolonged period of calm, a rich vegetation had covered the old layers of lava. The entire mass of Vesuvius was one luxuriant area, with its summit thick with woods where boar hunting was commonly practised along with the hunting of various types of game. The old storiography and the iconography confirms that the mountain was consecrated to Bacchus and was known above all for the excellent wines produced by the rich vineyards covering its lower slopes. On the wine amphoras taken from Pompeii it is still frequently possible to read the tag, "Vesuvinum", that is, "wine from Vesuvio", and in the Pompeian kitchens the heads of boars can still be seen in the frescoes.
Over the course of the centuries, the volcano's fury and the lack of care by man have often meant the entire area has been abandoned and degraded. But in spite of the fact that the slopes have often been overrun by lava flows the natural vegetation has always succeeded in reconquering those lost areas.
Today the volcano walls, in their upper parts, are covered with lapilli, pumice, scorie and black and reddish lava. Here, there is a marginal existence only for some algae, a bit of moss or lichen (typical here is the stereocaulo vesuviano), while a characteristic feature of the Vesuvian scenery which has never disappeared is "... the fragrant broom, happy in deserts...", celebrated by the great poet, Giacomo Leopardi. On the other hand, below this higher strip, nature offers one of its most varied and luxuriant displays. The more or less recent initiatives to protect the environment have lead to the setting up of the Vesuvian Nature Park and have promoted vast operations of reafforestation, while the thriving agricultural belt on the mountain slopes have for some time been a point of pride and wealth for the area. The precious vineyards which produce the famous "Lachryma Christi", the blossoming cultivation of orchards and fruit trees, the flowering exuberance of the stupendous gardens, the stretches of thick pine woods, all of this superabundance of fertility makes for such a striking contrast with the harsh and acrid sterility of the higher section, that unmistakable and so characteristic image of Vesuvius.

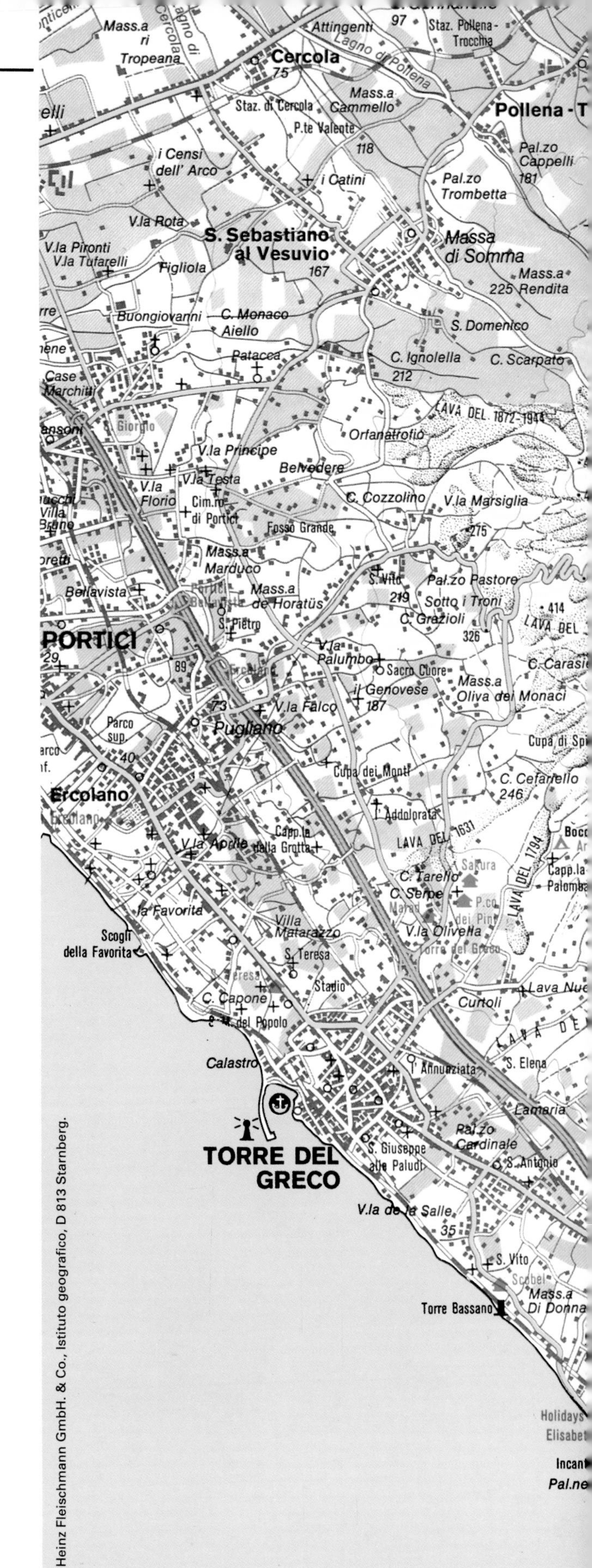


© Heinz Fleischmann GmbH. & Co., Istituto geografico, D 813 Starnberg.

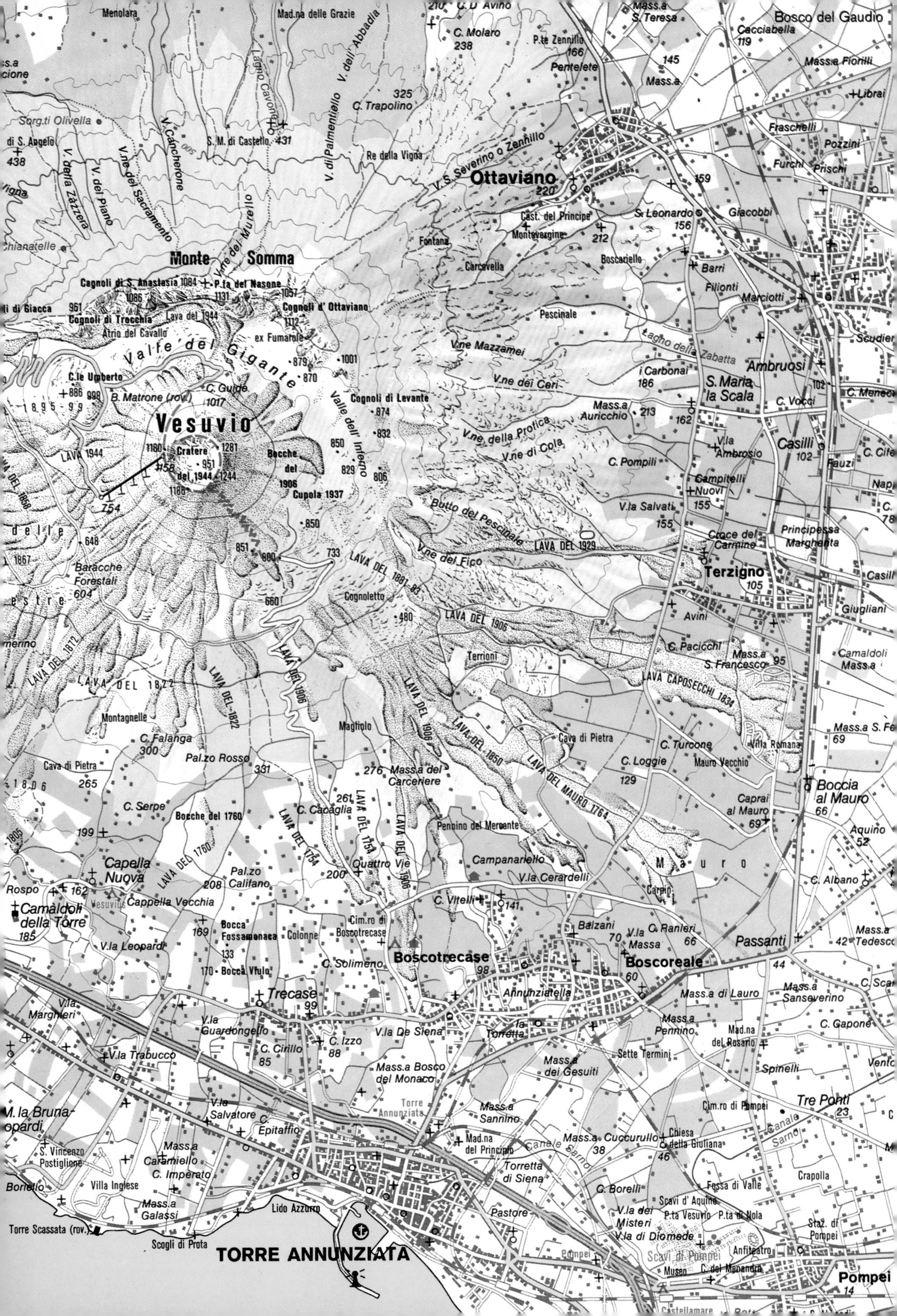

Menolara
Mad.na delle Grazie
C. D'Avino
Mass.a S. Teresa
Bosco del Gaudio
Cacciabella 119
C. Molaro 238
P.te Zennillo 166
Pentelete
145
Mass.a
Mass.a Fiorilli
Librai
Lagno Cavone
V. dell' Abbadia
325
C. Trapolino
Sorg.ti Olivella
V. di Palmentiello
Fraschelli
Pozzini
di S. Angelo 438
V. della Zazzera
V. del Piano
V.ne del Sacramento
V. Cancherone
S. M. di Castello 431
Re della Vigna
V. S. Severino o Zennillo
Ottaviano 220
159
Furchi
Prischi
V.ne del Murello
Cast. del Principe
Montevergine
212
S. Leonardo 156
Giacobbi
Chianatelle
Monte Somma
Fontana
Carcavella
Boscariello
Barri
Filionti
Marciotti
Cagnoli di S. Anastasia 1084
P.ta del Nasone 1131
1086
1057
Cognoli d' Ottaviano 1112
Cognoli di Trocchia
Lava del 1944
Atrio del Cavallo
ex Fumarole
Pescinale
Valle del Gigante
V.ne Mazzamei
Lagno della Zabatta
Ambruosi
879
1001
870
C.le Umberto 886
998
B. Matrone (rov.)
C. Guide 1017
V.ne dei Ceri
i Carbonai 186
S. Maria la Scala
Cognoli di Levante
874
Valle dell' Inferno
Mass.a Auricchio
213
162
C. Vocci
Vesuvio
832
V.ne della Profica
V.ne di Cola
V.la Ambrosio
Casilli 102
Fauzi
LAVA 1944
1180
Cratere 951
del 1944
1281
1244
1158
1186
Bocche del 1906
850
829
806
C. Pompili
Campitelli Nuovi 155
Cupola 1937
754
V.la Salvati 155
Butto del Pescinale
648
850
LAVA DEL 1929
Croce del Carmine
Principessa Margherita
1867
Baracche Forestali 604
851
800
733
V.ne del Fico
Terzigno 105
LAVA DEL 1881-83
660
Cognoletto
480
LAVA DEL 1906
Avini
Giugliani
LAVA DEL 1872
Terrioni
C. Pacicchi
Mass.a S. Francesco 95
Camaldoli Mass.a
LAVA DEL 1822
LAVA DEL 1906
LAVA CAPOSECCHI 1834
Montagnelle
Magliolo
LAVA DEL 1850
Cava di Pietra
C. Turcone
Villa Romana
Mass.a S. Fe 69
C. Falanga 300
Pal.zo Rosso
331
276
Mass.a del Carceriere
LAVA DEL MAURO 1764
C. Loggie 129
Mauro Vecchio
Cava di Pietra 265
Boccia al Mauro 66
C. Serpe
261
C. Cacaglia
LAVA DEL 1754
Caprai al Mauro 69
Bocche del 1760
Pennino del Mercante
Aquino 52
199
LAVA DEL 1760
LAVA DEL 1906
Campanariello
Mauro
Capella Nuova
Pal.zo Califano
208
200
Quattro Vie
V.la Cerardelli
C. Albano
Rospo
162
Cappella Vecchia
C. Vitelli
141
Carpin
Camaldoli della Torre 185
169
Bocca Fossamonaca
Colonne
Cim.ro di Boscotrecase
Balzani
70
V.la Massa
C. Ranieri 66
Passanti
Mass.a Tedesco 42
V.la Leopardi
133
C. Solimeno
Boscotrecase 98
Boscoreale 60
44
170
Bocca Vfulo
Trecase 99
Annunziatella
Mass.a di Lauro
Mass.a Sanseverino
V.la Marghieri
V.la Guardongello
V.la De Siena
la Torretta
Mass.a Pennino
Mad.na del Rosario
C. Gapone
C. Cirillo 85
C. Izzo 88
Sette Termini
V.la Trabucco
Mass.a Bosco del Monaco
Mass.a dei Gesuiti
Spinelli
M. la Bruna
V.la Salvatore
C. Epitaffio
Torre Annunziata
Mass.a Sannino
Cim.ro di Pompei
Tre Ponti 23
Mad.na del Principio
Mass.a Cuccurullo 38
Chiesa della Giuliana 46
Canale Sarno
S. Vincenzo Postiglione
Mass.a Caramiello
C. Imperato
Torretta di Siena
C. Borelli
Fossa di Valle
Crapolla
Villa Inglese
Mass.a Galassi
Lido Azzurro
Pastore
Scavi d' Aquino
V.la dei Misteri
P.ta Vesuvio
P.ta di Nola
V.la di Diomede
Staz. di Pompei
Torre Scassata (rov.)
Scogli di Prota
TORRE ANNUNZIATA
Scavi di Pompei
Anfiteatro
Museo
C. del Menandro
Pompei 14
Castellammare

# EXCURSIONS INTO VESUVIAN TERRITORY

**POMPEII**
The city of Pompeii occupied, before it was destroyed by Vesuvius, an area of around 66 hectares and the perimeter walls measured some 3,200 metres. Since it was built on the natural spur of a lava flow raised to some 40 metres above sea level, this inhabited area never had any regular urban development, having to adapt itself to the needs of the terrain, often characterised by steep slopes. The only flat part in the area was at the extreme north west and this was the area assigned to the Forum and the large public buildings.
At the present time the excavation works have made it possible to bring to light about seventy per cent of the urban structure, during the course of researche which, with alternating interruptions, has now lasted for more than two centuries. It was started indeed back in 1748 at the behest of the King, Carlo di Borbone, whose interest had been aroused by some fortuitous finds. The excavations proceeded for many years, very slowly and without any program. Yet notwithstanding the absence of any systematic criteria in the research, the spot constantly revealed its incredible richness in terms of the treasures hidden in its environs: in just over a century innumerable complexes came to light including the so-called Villa di Cicerone, the Via dei Sepolcri, the Villa di Diomede, the Theatre, Forum and the Basilica, the Temple of Fortune, the Public Baths, the Casa di Pansa, that of the Poeta Tragico, the Casa del Fauno and many many others. In the last century, after Italian unification, there was an attempt to apply some rigour to the scientific method with regard to the works, together with a careful conservation of the findings. The archaeological research techniques have been continuously refined and today their aim is to provide an integrated and, as far as possible, faithful view of the discoveries, with the restoration of the architectonic elements and the conservation of the original decoration and the artistic and domestic furnishings.
The urban structure appears to be the classical Roman settlement layout, with rectilinear and right-angled roads (the cardines and decumani) and walkways paved with Vesuvian stone. Frequently, at the road junctions, there are the remains of the old public fountains and even the altars dedicated to the public cult of the Lares. The inscriptions are many and intriguing, as are the drawings traced on the walls of the houses and the public buildings, covering various subjects: from the love dedication to insults. The number of the shops is

*Arresting image of the Vesuvian mountain as seen from the villages along the coastal strip . In the foreground the lava flow that destroyed San Sebastiano in 1944*

*Reconstruction of the Vesuvian area at the time of the Roman Empire, showing the largest towns in the area during the eruption in 79 BC*

*Pompeii, Villa of Mysteries - The sacrifice, and Silenus playing his instrument*

*Partial panoramic view of the excavations in Pompeii with a central view of the Forum*

considerable and there is no shortage of their signs, be they painted or sculptured. In addition there are the hostels, stables, the private and public baths. Amid the dense network of private habitations there are three centres of public, religious and civil life: the Forum square with the most important temple in the city, the Theatre district, the Amphitheatre and the Great Gymnasium. Exceptional evidence of the luxury and the refinement of Pompeii, its buildings are among the most complete and impressive in existence, silent witnesses to an ancient way of life.

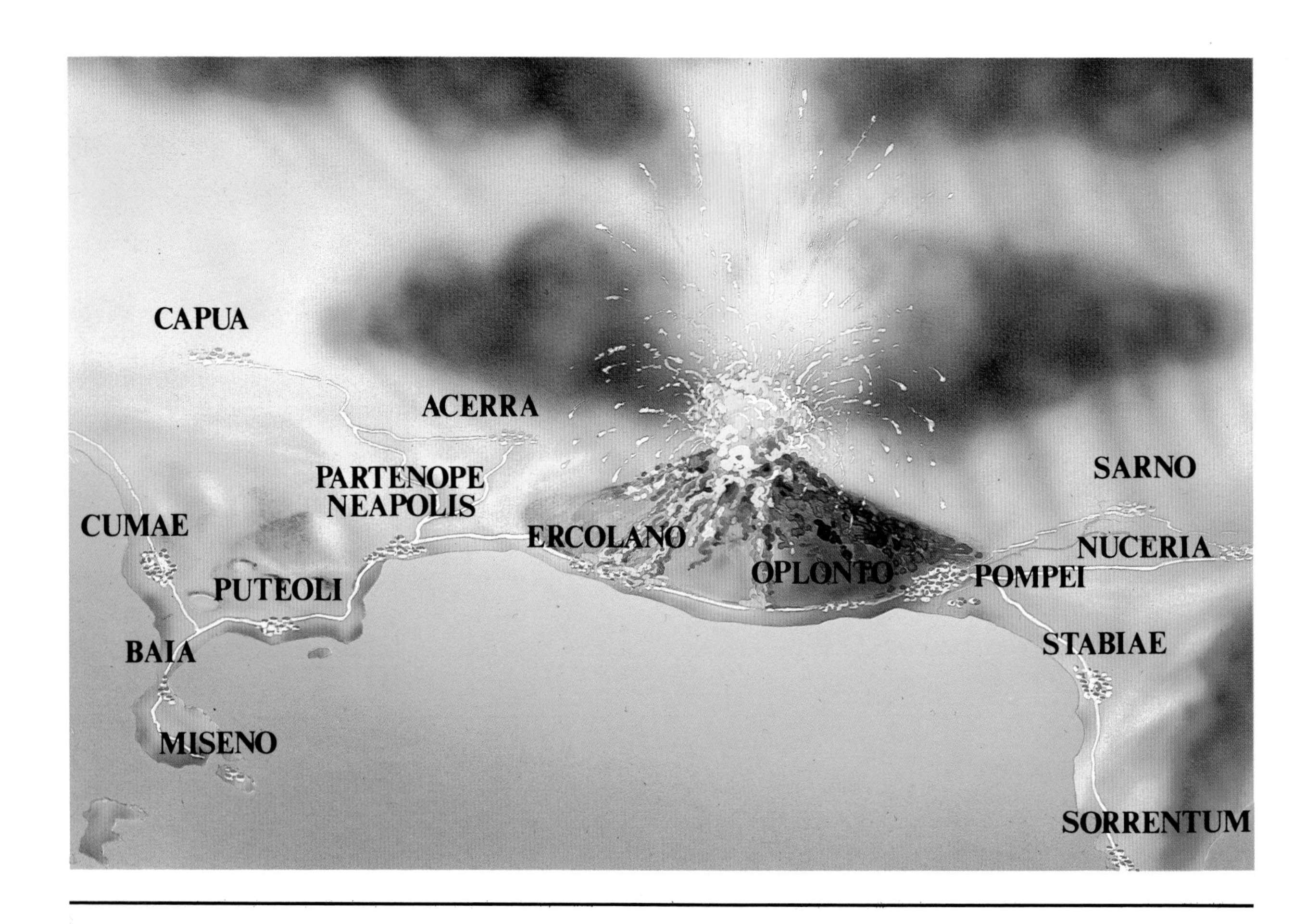

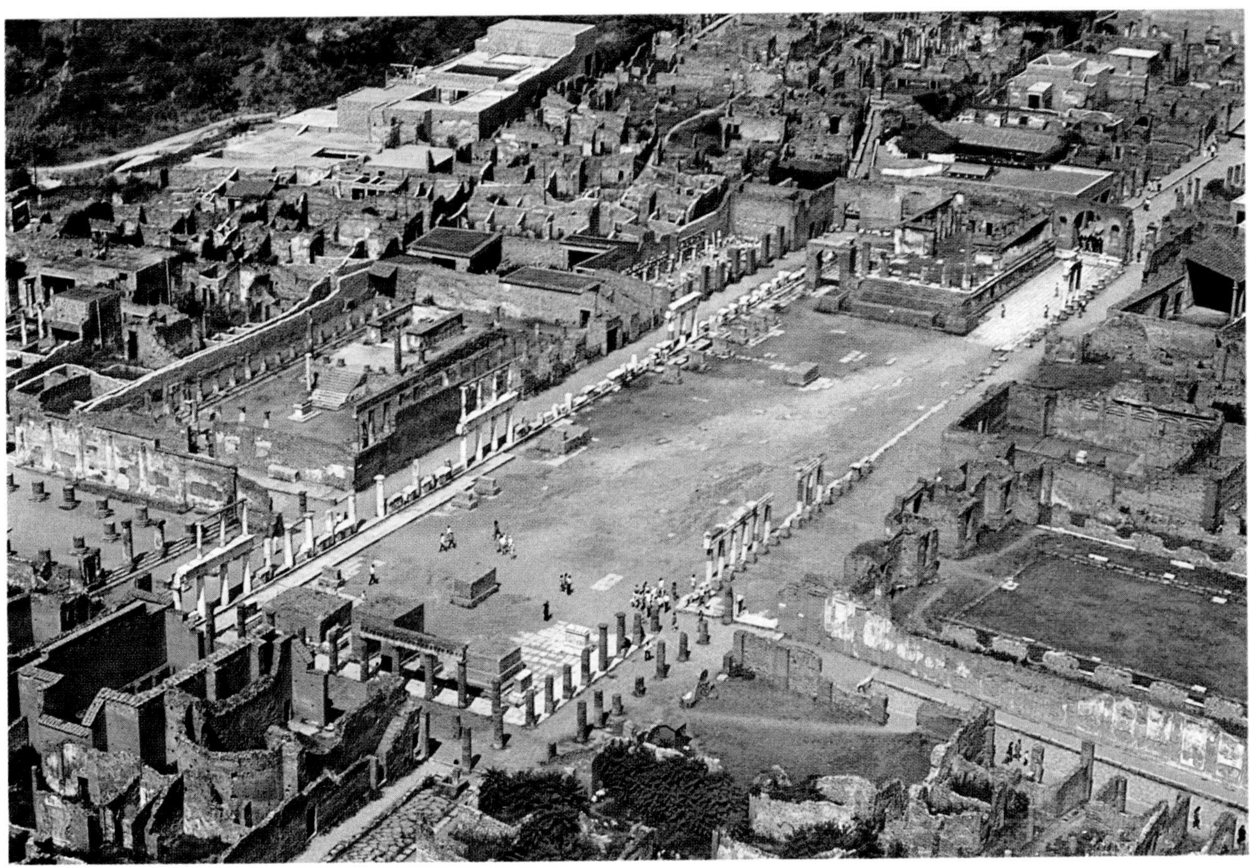

*Pages 56/57*
*Aerial view of the excavations and impressions of bodles discovered in a garden*

*Interior of the house containing the mosaic of Neptune and Amphitrite, at Herculaneum: the mosaic decoration is clearly visible to the right*

*Drunken satyr with a wineskin, a statue discovered and preserved in the Casa dei Cervi at Herculaneum*

*Drunken satyr in the act of urinating, one of the most realistic examples of Herculaneum's many sculptural riches*

*Partial shot of the crossroad formed by the Cardo and the Decumano, the two main streets at Herculaneum*

## HERCULANEUM

According to legend it was founded by Hercules on his return from his fabulous travels in Iberia. The town rises up on the extreme spurs of a promontory which from the slopes of Vesuvius pushes out into the sea. The deep courses of the two torrents which run along both sides of this city provided it with two convenient natural ports. When it was buried by the destructive eruption of the volcano in 79 AD the city had between four and five thousand inhabitants. Even though, within its walls, its opulence and wealth was no match for that at Pompeii, the refinement and vigour of its craftwork attracted numerous noble families, with their particularly sophisticated traditions and tastes, who set up their sumptuous villas amid the the surrounding areas.
Started some two centuries ago, in 1738, again at the command of the enlightened King, Carlo di Borbone, the excavation works at Herculaneum have undergone vicissitudes and interruptions on many more, and under more stressful conditions, than those at nearby Pompeii and they have been relaunched in a continuous fashion only since 1927. Carried out in recent years using modern criteria and techniques, the work has only partially brought to light the area of ancient habitation which to a large extent still lies buried under the more populated districts of today's Resina.
The work carried out in this century has provided results of extreme importance, allowing the recovery of entire inhabited districts and various public buildings: from the Forum, the centre of economic, social and political life in the city, to the distinctive architecture of the Public Baths. Although considerably smaller than nearby Pompeii, Herculaneum is today one of the most

INSVLA V

*Complete panoramic shot of the excavation works at Herculaneum*

interesting archaeological complexes of Roman antiquity. The urban and structural details recovered provide a glimpse of a social reality entirely different from that at Pompeii: the roads, for example, paved with Vesuvian stone and in calcareous rock, do not show any signs of deep ruts that would indicate heavy traffic nor are there the large stones which usually facilitated crossing from one side to the other; mural inscriptions, too, are rare. Very few human victims have been found. The houses reveal a greater variety of types, with buildings having more floors and habitations, something very rare in the architecture of the time. The superior conservation of the Herculaneum houses, due to the special circumstances of their burial, makes it possible to understand with greater precision their distinctive character. Since it was without doubt a non-industrial and commercial city the contrast here between the patrician and common houses is so much clearer. The most important of these noble houses to be discovered is undoubtedly the so-called Villa dei Papiri, where the rich and cultured owner had collected a library of almost two thousand parchments, for the most part concerning philosophy. To this can be added the grandiose theatre and the monumental Basilica, as well as the Mater Deum temple and the Public Baths. Particularly interesting is the study of the residential quarters, arranged according to a highly balanced urban plan, clearly under strong Greek influence. Life in

*Partial shot of the interior portico in the Villa di Oplonti*

Herculaneum was therefore pursued in an atmosphere of refined Hellenistic culture, amid dignified and noble luxury.

## OPLONTI

If Herculaneum calls to mind, understandably, residences used exclusively for the holidays (otium) by a privileged class, not ever far away and closer to the opulent and chaotic Pompeii, in an entrancing bay on the coast, in the shelter of today's hamlet of Torre Annunziata, are the largest and most sumptuous remains of the suburban villas. The ancient name of this spot, Oplonti, was found in the so-called Tavola Peutingeriana, that is, one of the rarest geographical charts to have it come down to us from the ancient world, showed showing the most important communication routes in the Empire, with the stations and large centres marked with special symbols. The putative drafting date for the Tavola Peutingeriana lies between the second and fourth century AD. Thus Oplonti, about which there a refern historical references, must have been perfecty untegrated before this period, perfectly integrated and certainly of considerable importance.

The two grandiose architectural complexes, now almost entirely uncovered, the so-called Casa di Poppea and the Villa di Crasso, bear witness to a special custom in

*Details of the excavations and several examples of the highly refined pictorial decorations in the Villa di Oplonti*

the society of that time which had evidently found its perfect setting at Oplonti.
The phenomenon of the villa is specific to Roman culture, determined by the way social life was organised and by the traditional, conscious distinction between work and leisure time (the first understood as public activity, the second as otium, that is care of the body and the spirit). From this point of view it is easy to understand the tight and binding relation existing between the villa and the surrounding natural environment, a relation with a determining effect on its architectural structure. And though this also evolved over time in diversified forms and was at times clearly innovative, the Roman villa always has its roots in the two classical and traditional types, which draw on a single initial unit: the rural villa, the centre of the agricultural unit, and the great urban complex, typical of the imperial period. In the first, around the porticoed central courtyard on to which the living quarters opened, there are also the service quarters and those assigned to agricultural work (the barn, cellars, granary). In the second type there are more in the accessory areas (from the four-sided portico to the library, baths).
The two monumental complexes found at Oplonti clearly show the evolution of this tradition.
The Villa di Poppea, (perhaps Poppea Sabina, Nero's second wife), is made up of around one hundred areas and includes an olympic-size swimming pool decorated with statues.
In addition to a precious collection of necklaces, jewels and valuable objects these areas have revealed, a very rich collection of sculptures. The mural decoration in the

rooms is clearly related to the second Pompeian style, the first century BC, which, features the representation of architecture in perspective, and stretching over the walls are sceneries including buildings, complete with colonnades, friezes and pediments, framing lively human or countryside images.
Not far from the grandiose example of Poppea there is the Villa di Crasso, a rich vine-grower. Here the rural spaces, set out with ample spaces and structures, reveal the different functions, as still suggested today by the four hundred amphoras (with their musk inside) preserved on site and by the heaps of pomegranates, probably left out to dry.
As with Herculaneum and Pompeii, Oplonti too has an exceptionally important place in historical reconstruction, particularly with regard to art indeed it comprises indeed one of the most complex and impressive nuclei of what was, two thousand years ago, the Roman world. Beyond its architectural or sculptural finds, which are in themseoves incredibly precious, the almost complete absence elsewhere of Roman pictorial remains (as with Greek pictorial art) makes the discovery of this complex supremely important.

## INDEX




© 1992 - KINA ITALIA S. p. A. - Milan


Distributed by IL GIRASOLE SOUVENIR srl - Phone: 081/5592080
Production and printing - KINA ITALIA S. p. A. - Milan
Translation by ATD Milan
Lay-out by Renzo Matino


All rights for texts and photographs reserved.
Reproduction including partial reproduction forbidden.



**L. 8000**

*Photographic library : Vesuvian Notebooks - Bruno Faraone (Architect )*